RELATIONSHIP
AND
VALUE SYSTEM

*A Guide to Successful
and
Happy Relationships*

Darren Twa

BlackStripes Publishing

© 2009 Darren Twa

BlackStripes Publishing
19814 55th Avenue NE
Kenmore, WA 98028-3198

Relationship and Value System:
A Guide to Successful and Happy Relationships
ISBN 978-0-9823574-2-2

All rights reserved. No part of this book may be reproduced, stored in a retrieval system, or transmitted in any form or by any means—electronic, mechanical, photocopy, recording, or otherwise—except for brief quotations for the purpose of review or comment, without the prior permission of the publisher.

Contents

1 Relationships are based on common value systems   1

2 All conflict in relationship is conflict over values   7

3 Three areas of desire that affect your values   13

4 Conflict is resolved by agreeing on values   21

5 Sacrificial love as a value system   31

6 Communicating what you value   37

7 Becoming a sacrificial lover   43

1 Relationships are based on common value systems

Your value system is the sum total of your ideas and beliefs. It includes every opinion you hold about life. Each thing you like or dislike, and the importance each one has to you, merges to form your unique value system.

Your value system develops through what you are taught and experience, combined with your reactions to them, forming your preferences and your unique perspective on life. Ultimately, *every opinion you have in life is based on something in your value system.*

No two people completely share the

same value system because our values are more than our moral beliefs. They are also shaped by our preferences for kinds of food, our hobbies, and types of entertainment. Not everything in a person's value system is a matter of right or wrong. Some of what we like or dislike is absolutely non-moral.

We can develop relationships around non-moral values, such as our hobbies and entertainment. However, in order to have strong relationships with others, we need to have certain values in common. Most significantly, our moral values must be as similar as possible.

The quality of any relationship is directly linked to the *importance* of the shared values. Two people may share a common interest in football, but if one thinks the other is a liar and a thief, they likely will not develop a deep friendship. On the other hand, if we have a mutual interest in keeping our neighborhood safe, our views on sports will not interfere with our working together for that common goal.

Relationships grow over time as the participants grow together in their values. When two people meet for the first time, they do not know very much about what the other person values. Each one makes assumptions about the other, some of which are true while others are false. Yet, over time, if they discover that they agree on their most important values, their relationship will deepen and grow stronger.

This is also true regarding all family relationships. Parents usually seek to instill their values into their children. As a child grows, she forms her own unique value system. She either rejects or retains her parents values, and she chooses how much influence each value will have in her own life. The quality of the relationship the parent and child share is completely dependent on how much they agree on each other's *most significant* values.

Relationships are based on common values systems and you experience this truth every day. You want to be with those who share your interests and moral ideas. Conversely, you avoid people who do not share values similar to yours, whether in moral areas of life or simply in manners or interests. In fact, it is difficult to enjoy a relationship with someone who is substantially different from you.

Of course, the true values that we hold are the ones by which we actually live. If we claim to value something, yet do the opposite of it, then we actually value something else. If I claim to value truth, yet lie, then there is something more important to me than telling the truth. My lies prove that I hold some other value more deeply than honesty.

Every family has rules or expectations of what each member should or should not do. The degree to which we follow those expectations reveals how much we agree with them. Although we might not agree on a rule or expectation, we might still live according to it in order to preserve our family relationships. In that case, we value the relationship as more important than choosing our own rules and having our own way.

Our actions are the first indicators to ourselves and others about the values we hold because the values that we live by are connected to what is most important to us. However, we can sometimes have other desires in our hearts that differ from our actions. To be completely at peace within yourself, there must be conformity between your deepest values and how you actually live. That is, you must be committed to your deepest values and seek to live according to them. Otherwise, you will experience inner conflict because you have not determined which values are most important to you, and every choice you make will not flow from a firmly held belief about that area of life.

This inner conflict is sometimes revealed through your emotions. When you struggle in making an important decision, it might be because you do not have a firm value about it, or because you lack the information you need to match it to the values you hold. From strongly held values comes a greater ability to make choices in life.

Experiencing emotion that you enjoy (such as happiness) is an indication that you are obtaining what you value. Getting what you want and having things done your way results in satisfaction and pleasure. *Emotions reveal your values.* The stronger you feel an emotional response, the more important the value is to you that is being fulfilled.

Although any fulfillment of our values can feel good, our greatest happiness comes from experiencing positive emotions that fulfill our values in the context of relationship. Relationships that make us happy are based on common values and are enjoyable, satisfying, and fulfilling. To experience them, we need to understand ourselves and connect deeply with one another.

2 All conflict in relationship is conflict over value system

Whenever you experience a disagreement with someone, it is always a disagreement over one of your values. That is, you see the matter one way, and the other person sees it another way. It may be something trivial or something extremely important to you, but all conflict in relationship is conflict over value system.

That which we agree on draws us closer together, whereas disagreement drives us apart. The more important something is to you—the more you value it—the greater the conflict you will have when someone disagrees with you or obstructs your plans. This conflict over value system is the destructive factor in *all* relationships.

When a person first feels "in love," one aspect of the emotion flows from strong beliefs about the *other* person's value system. We tend to believe that the other person values the same things we do. However, as the relationship progresses, we begin to realize that we do not share all the values we first anticipated. It is during these times of disappointment or conflict that we discover the real values of one another. As the illusion of common values breaks down, so do some of the positive emotions.

Although we want our relationships only to produce happiness, we know that they do not. Conflict in relationship produces fear that we will be rejected because of our values. Therefore, we begin to hide our true desires from others, which produces feelings of loneliness even in the midst of relationship.

We often desire to freely express who we really are to another person—even if only one other person. The expression of who we are is a full revelation of our deepest values. Not only do we want to be open and honest about who we are and what we desire, we also want to be accepted as we are. Although we know there are parts of us that need improvement, we do not want to be criticized as we seek to change our lives to match our highest virtues. We imagine the perfect relationship to be one where we can openly share the deepest desires of our hearts and yet never experience rejection for what we are.

Conflict in relationship is conflict over value system and we experience it frequently. Every quarrel or fight is a battle over whose value will prevail. It may be as trivial as deciding which movie to watch, or as severe as quitting your job because your boss treats you badly.

You even experience conflict with those you love whenever their desires do not match yours. As long as you both agree, you do not have conflict because you are living a shared value system. But each time you disagree, the magnitude of the dispute is related to how important the current issue is to you. The level of conflict is directly proportional to the significance each of you place on the value over which you disagree.

Experiencing emotions that you do not enjoy (such as sadness or anger) is an indication that your values are not being fulfilled. You feel negative emotion when you are not getting what you want and are not having things done your way. When people or situations do not meet your expectations, you experience your values as an expression of your emotions. The stronger you sense these negative feelings, the more significant the values underlying them are to you.

It is important to note that emotions are only a response to whether or not your values are being accomplished. Many people attempt to stop being angry without understanding and dealing with its source: the *value conflict* between them and another person. Until the real issue is dealt with, feelings of anger will not be kept in check.

When you prolong conflict in relationship, it demonstrates that what you value is *more important to you than the relationship*. You would rather have your own way than have the relationship progress and improve; and, if you cannot have your own way, then you are willing to let the relationship degrade. People argue because they have different values from each other, and unless they view the relationship as more important than the subject of conflict, they will be more willing to dissolve it rather than resolve their differences in value system.

For example, couples often disagree about money and how it should be earned, spent, or saved. Each idea they have flows from something deep within. It may be because they want the pleasure of spending it or the security of saving it. Therefore, when a couple disagrees about money, they need to be able to understand and express the values driving their desires and feelings. If they cannot come to an agreement on values, they need to at least agree that their relationship is more important to them than their choice in how to spend money. Hopefully, from the greater value they place on relationship will come the means by which to resolve their lesser values concerning money.

If we truly desire to have good relationships, we need to resolve conflicts by changing our values. Some of your values will need to change as well as some of the other person's. We will not agree on how important everything in life is, but to grow closer we must agree on the values we deem most significant.

We must also feel acceptance when we express our values. If we cannot share the deepest values of our hearts and still be accepted, then the relationship will never bring us the fulfillment we desire. We will continue to have conflict with each other because, without openness, we will not understand the values that are really producing the conflict.

Lying is destructive to relationship because lying is pretending to share a common value system without actually agreeing on it. It wants the *benefits* of relationship without truly sharing the values that produce relationship. People often lie in order to prevent conflict, but they only produce more once their dishonesty and hypocrisy are discovered.

Good relationships can only be formed by sharing your true values. To be accepted and liked for values that you are only pretending to possess is not real relationship, and it will never bring deep fulfillment. If values you hold are interfering with your relationships, you need to choose whether you would rather improve your relationships or keep your current values.

3 Three areas of desire that affect your values

Before you can resolve conflicts in your life, you must first understand how your value system is ordered. Although emotions reveal what you desire, you also need to understand the nature of all your desires. All of your values—from the least to the greatest—are shaped by three main areas of desire: your bodily appetites, what you want people to think about you, and your personal kingdom (wealth, possessions, and control).

You have many desires simply because you need to care for your body. These include basic cleanliness, air, and food. But you also have the need to be touched and held in positive, loving ways, as well as desires for sexual fulfillment. How important these desires are will vary from person to person, but they are common to all and our choices in life depend on how much we value each appetite.

Most of us are at least partially motivated by the desire to have others like or approve of us. The more important a relationship is to us, the more we try to please the other in that relationship. We also try to conform to the values held by the group with which we want to be associated. It is not uncommon for people to do or say that which will positively affect their reputations, even if it is something they do not really mean.

We also tend to avoid doing anything that will cause us to be rejected. We may act our part, knowing that negative words or actions will result from our holding different values. This occurs in families, the workplace, and also in social groups. We desperately want to be accepted, and the desire for relationship strongly shapes many of our values. Whenever we speak or act in order to impress others, or have them like or adore us, we demonstrate this reality. If the desire to be accepted by others is so strong that we are compelled to act against other values that we hold, we experience inner conflict.

For example, a child may want his friends to accept him even if they require him to do something he believes is wrong to become part of the group. The reason he feels inner turmoil is because he is attempting to live by two conflicting values. Ultimately, the value that he considers most important will prevail. Experiencing painful consequences for non-conformity results in adults who also feel anxiety should they differ from others during social situations.

Having people like us is also the desire behind how we dress or present ourselves. A woman who deems it very important to appear beautiful in the eyes of others will expend money and energy in achieving that goal. It is not wrong to look attractive, but it is important to understand the values within that make it such an important issue.

Finally, we desire to have what we want when we want it. It may be about wealth, possessions, or simply having our own will be done. This desire often appears as a need to be in control, but it also appears as rebellion against authority.

When a couple has different ideas of how

money should be spent it often relates to issues of security or fairness. They will argue over who spends more pleasing oneself, or they may feel cheated if they do not get to purchase what they prefer. This conflict happens in families, in business, and in government. All of us want to have wealth used to achieve our own plans.

The values in our hearts produce emotions based on whether or not our values are being satisfied. When our desires in these three areas (bodily appetites, having people like us, and obtaining wealth and power) are fulfilled we usually feel happy. However, when we do not achieve our desires and goals we feel miserable and upset. We become angry and frustrated when life does not turn out the way we expect, whether in our relationships at home or in difficulties at work. Our desires for ease of life, in having others do what we wish, or in having possessions that we believe will make us happy profoundly affect our relationships.

These three areas of desire are natural and there is nothing wrong with them; however, our expressions of them can either enhance or destroy our relationships. Since all of our values and desires affect relationship, and since our greatest happiness comes from good relationships, we should seek a value system that enhances rather than detracts from relationship. Consider the following examples that show how our values and desires affect our relationships.

We all share the common bodily appetite for food, but it can become an issue of overeating. On the one hand I value eating reasonable portions of healthy food, yet on the other hand I value eating as much as I can of tasty cuisine. Often these two values conflict. My true value is the one that I live. If I live according to my second value, I will gain weight and my relationships will suffer. I will be concerned about what my spouse and others think about me, and I may not have the energy to play with my children.

We also share bodily appetites for physical touching. However, if I do not control and limit whom I touch and how I touch them, there will be profound consequences. Without strong values limiting my desires, my relationships will suffer or be destroyed.

Everyone wants to be positively regarded by others, yet many children seek acceptance from their peers by doing activities that they know their parents disapprove of. We cannot please everyone, so while attempting to gain approval by some, we often alienate others. Our deepest values will determine whose attention we will seek and which relationships we will sacrifice to gain recognition.

We tend to think that our own ideas are better than the ideas of others, so we often want others to do what we desire. However, in pressing for control, we can cause people to dislike us and our attitudes. Whenever I demand to have my way, I damage the relationships with those I am seeking to control.

People driven to gain great wealth or possessions often do so at the expense of others. If we exploit others to become rich, we will gain a reputation that will haunt all of our relationships. If I spend my family's income to purchase toys for myself without regard for the needs of my spouse or children, they will resent my selfishness. Alternatively, if I use my wealth to help others, it will create or enhance my relationships with them.

All three areas of desire affect relationship. The values we hold either make our relationships stronger or tear them apart. Unless we evaluate the positive and negative affects they have, we will fail to resolve conflicts. If I choose to live by desires that destroy my relationships, it reveals how much I value myself more than others. In order to have quality relationships, I must share the same positive values that are held by those I love.

4 Conflict is resolved by agreeing on values

Since all conflict in relationship is conflict over value system, the only way to remove conflict is by agreeing on values. Not all conflict over value system is relationally destructive. Usually only moral issues and excessive indulgence in non-moral desires have a negative impact on relationship. But where the conflicting values are hindering or damaging a relationship, only a change of value can restore and improve the relationship. Until one or both people change and agree to live by a common value system there will continue to be conflict.

There are four steps in resolving conflict

and repairing damaged relationships. Both parties involved in the conflict must participate willingly because the steps are shared between the people involved. The four steps are like the wheels on a car: if you want a smooth ride you need all four in place.

Resolving conflict requires agreement on value system, so each step involved relates to a change in values. The value producing the conflict must be altered, and there must be agreement on how each person should now act toward the other. Furthermore, problems created by the previous value system must not be allowed to hinder the progressing relationship.

Step 1: Confession:
Admitting your fault

People need to admit when they are wrong. Unless at least one person is willing to admit that he made a mistake or was acting in a way that was damaging the relationship, there will be no progress in improving the relationship. Without verbal acknowledgement that an action was wrong, there will be an obstruction in that area of the relationship.

Admitting fault is a declaration that the relationship cannot be built around a conflict-producing value. It is the first step in coming to an agreement on value system because it is an acknowledgement that my particular value was wrong and yours was right. When I admit my fault, I am admitting *my* value caused the problem and that *my* value needs to change in order to resolve the problem.

Sometimes we do realize that what we did was wrong, and we may even try to change how we live. However, if we do not express that to the person we mistreated, our relationship with him accumulates negative emotional pain that is not removed. Only by admitting our fault can we bring relief and positive emotion to the one we have hurt.

It is humbling to admit we were wrong, but we gain greater strength to change once we openly admit we were the one at fault. Humility makes us stronger, and we need that strength to build a stronger relationship based on better values.

Step 2: Repentance: Replacing your values

Confession is verbalizing the problem, whereas *repentance is changing the value that produced the problem.* When we repent of a value that has been harming a relationship, we change the way we act so that we do not hurt the other person again in this same way. Without change, the conflict will certainly re-emerge because the difference in value system has not been resolved. Only an agreement on values brings two people together and prepares for a future without ongoing conflict in this area.

Repentance is a promise to live by a new value in the area that was producing conflict. It is a living admission that the value and the relational damage it produced are interconnected. New values bring hope that the relationship will be better than it was before. The genuineness of repentance is always demonstrated through permanent change.

Step 3: Forgiveness: Removing the relational consequences of the offence

Once the person (whose actions were the source of the conflict) has confessed and pledged change, the person who was hurt needs to forgive. Forgiveness is a promise you make to the one who has hurt you that you will not punish him for what he has done. Of course, this forgiveness is for the betterment of the relationship.

With forgiveness, the relationship receives a new starting point subsequent to the conflict. Because the person's value that produced the conflict has now changed, the forgiver must not treat the person according to his *previous* value system. In a sense, the old person is gone and a new and better person is there to love.

Forgiveness is not an issue of how we feel since it operates independently from our emotions. However, once a person has truly confessed and repented, the forgiver will have an easier time recovering emotionally from any grievance. Until the feelings of hurt diminish, we need to act according to a value that loves, forgives, and is glad the other person has changed. When we forgive we must not recall memories of an offense in order to harm or punish the other.

Forgiveness is treating a person according to his new value system and not his old one, although some deeds may have consequences requiring further action. Yet, in terms of relationship, both people are no longer at odds. Seeking forgiveness is always about the desire to have a relationship restored; it is never merely a means to avoid punishment for what one has done.

In order to truly forgive someone, you must not seek to get even with him before he asks for forgiveness; instead, you must wait for him to repent. Taking revenge on someone makes true forgiveness impossible—for you have already made that person pay. Revenge contributes to the destruction of a relationship and proves that you also have values that need to change. Any harm you bring against another person before or after he asks forgiveness will require you to confess and repent of your wrongdoing.

It may be necessary to discuss the issue with the other person so that he understands how his actions have damaged the relationship. However, gently focus on values rather than on emotions or desires when attempting to produce change in the other person. Otherwise, he may have a tendency to feel attacked and resist hearing what you have to say.

Step 4: Reconciliation:
Restoring the relationship

The last step in resolving conflict is restoration of the relationship. Even when people have changed and forgiven, sometimes it is difficult to "go on" in the relationship. Sometimes this is because of embarrassment and sometimes this is because of a history of many painful experiences. Whatever the reason, people often prefer to turn away from one another rather than have the relationship improve. This is most unfortunate because they are now at a turning point to experience a better relationship than ever before.

Reconciliation between two people who previously experienced conflict is the fullest sign that they understand how important their relationship is. Instead of dwelling on the past painful conflict, they recognize that a closer relationship can now form because *they now have more agreement on their values.* All relationships are based on common values, and one of the deepest values two people need to share is the importance of pursuing relationship even beyond the difficult times.

Let me illustrate this process with a story. Imagine I am in the habit of leaving a mess in the kitchen and I expect my wife to clean up after me. Of course, she finds this frustrating; and, since she has told me numerous times not to do it, it is negatively affecting our relationship.

It is not enough for me to simply stop leaving a mess. Rather, I first need to acknowledge that my behavior has been wrong and selfish. Doing this will alleviate much of the tension my wife is feeling toward me. I then need to ask her to forgive me for reducing her to the role of a maid. The reality is that I had not valued her as I ought to have.

If I am sincere, I will now change my value system from one that permits me to leave messes for others to clean up to one that cleans up after myself. However, if I do not change, then my words were merely a ruse to avoid conflict. I may even fool myself into thinking I really meant them, but how I *live* proves the real values I hold. Confession without repentance only artificially removes the conflict and results in greater damage later.

Once I have confessed and asked for forgiveness, my wife can now tell by my words that I recognize the *values* that were producing the problem. Furthermore, my promise to work at changing them encourages her to forgive me and not to treat me according to how my old values deserved. Rather, she will treat me as though I have always picked up after myself.

My response to this beautiful gift she has given me is to thank her and do my best not to fail her. Our relationship is better because I have changed and we now agree on a common value, but also because she has forgiven me and will not punish me in some way for my previous actions.

A long-term relationship that has gone through struggles of change and openness can produce two people who have deep commitment and love for one another. They also learn to have freedom and openness in sharing their values, dreams, and desires. People whose relationships fall apart because of conflict never experience this deep joy.

If this process of resolving conflict does not make the relationship stronger, then some portion of it has been left undone: one of the steps has been avoided. Even as you would not like to drive your car if it were missing one of its wheels, so also each one of these four steps must be accomplished. Both people must be involved and committed to the relationship. They cannot quit out of embarrassment, resentment, or fear. If the relationship diminishes it is ultimately because someone still does not share the common value of how important *this* relationship is.

5 Sacrificial love as a value system

Conflict in relationship can be removed by agreement on values, but something more is required. We must not only agree on common values; we must also choose to live by a value system that contributes positively to relationship. The value system that produces the strongest relationships is one based on sacrificial love for others.

By seeking to serve those I love, my relationships regain a focus on how I am connected to others rather than focusing only on how I might fulfill my individual desires. The whole concept of relationship revolves around joining people together rather than separating them. Instead of focusing on what I want, I must consider the needs of the other person.

Sacrificial love demands my willingness to give up one of my own desires in order to fulfill a desire of the other person. If you truly love someone, and want her to know and feel it, you need to do what she values. As she does your values to you, you also will feel loved. Instead of two people each trying to make themselves happy regardless of the effect it has on others, they will find a two-fold happiness. First, they will experience the happiness brought into their lives by the other person loving them. Second, they will experience an additional happiness because of how they are making another person happy.

Sacrificial love for the benefit of others is also the best value system for producing and sustaining relationship because it has conflict reduction and resolution built-in. If two people are both trying to please the other rather than only pleasing one's self, it removes conflict. Desires that we might selfishly be attempting to fulfill in spite of their effect on the other person are eliminated. If I consider the effect my words and actions will have, I will be careful not to inflict pain or injury on anyone else. Rather than harming others, I will say and do things to make their lives better.

Sacrificial love cannot be artificial. You cannot merely "give in" to the desire of the other person. It must be the true value of your heart to serve. You must desire to please the other and build the relationship more than always having your own way. If it is merely an act, you will become frustrated when you are not served as you desire. Sacrificial love done only for what you will receive in return is not sacrificial love at all. That is why it only works in relationships with both participants seeking this same amazing value system.

Sacrificial love for the benefit of others must become the foundation of your value system. It does not necessarily eliminate your other interests or desires, unless they are selfish and contrary to love. But used as your most basic moral guide it will govern your other values and desires. Instead of considering all of the things you should or should not do, you only need to think of whether or not your actions and desires agree or conflict with sacrificial love. If what you desire conflicts with sacrificial love, you can be certain that it will also negatively affect your relationships.

It is like having the perfect ability to evaluate all aspects of relationship with one simple tool. However, you must be vigilant in examining your values and desires to see if they correspond with sacrificial love. If they do, and your partner in relationship is also being motivated by sacrificial love, then your relationship will flourish.

For example, let us consider actions that many people consider to be wrong. Murder, lying, and stealing are wrong because they are not sacrificial. However, instead of a list of negative rules, we can be guided by one positive value. Sacrificial love promotes doing good to others rather than merely avoiding doing harm to them. Anything that harms our relationships likely flows from some value that is opposed to sacrificial love.

This kind of relationship requires both parties to be committed to sacrificial love for the other. Without that commitment, the sacrificial lover will be exploited. Exploitation always destroys relationship, whereas sacrificial love enhances it. Exploitation is the opposite of sacrificial love. If we seek to fulfill our desires by using other people, we will hurt them and destroy our relationships. Whenever we force or manipulate others to serve us, we are exploiting them. People often use anger, threats, sulking, or crying as weapons when they cannot use physical force.

Therefore, it is crucially important that both people in a relationship be committed to sacrificially loving and forgiving each other when they are offended. Any attempt to hold on to a grudge will damage a relationship as much as selfishly having others serve you. This sacrificial love is tied to forgiveness in that it is willing not to punish the other person for what he has done. Instead of revenge, it prefers to restore relationship and to have the other person change his values. Sacrificial love is tied to repentance in that it is willing to give up a selfish desire in order to benefit the other person.

The greatest source of happiness we can have in life is relational. Although we can find pleasure in bodily appetites and in a personal kingdom, nothing fulfills us like having others truly love us. Therefore, it makes sense to pursue sacrificial love in our relationships so that we, along with those we love, can find deepest personal fulfillment.

6 Communicating what you value

Although you might spend a lot of time with someone, you may not know her deeply nor care to. This is not what most people would consider a good and healthy relationship. Before you can fulfill the desires of another person, you must understand her values and desires. Similarly, she also needs to know what is important to you. This requires openness and honesty, and a willingness to accept what you learn about the other person.

Truly knowing someone requires that you understand what is important to her. A person's value system shapes her character and affects all of her decisions. With a minimal or false idea of what a person's desires are, you will be unable to love her in ways that make her feel loved.

For a relationship to deepen, both participants must be willing to discover the values of the other person. As we learn these values, we will discover how much we are like or unlike the other. Where we differ, we must at least attempt to understand the other person's desires. If those desires are non-moral and thus not opposed to sacrificial love, we should be careful not to respond in a negative way. It might take time for a person to feel the freedom to share who he truly is, but an atmosphere of acceptance prepares him for greater exposure. Without the freedom to open up and be discovered, we cannot please one another and our relationship will suffer from superficiality.

Until a relationship moves to conversation about values, you may find that you are not truly communicating. Even if you talk about your wants and desires, you still might not fully understand yourself or what you are wanting of the other person. If you are speaking or acting from emotion then you might not be doing what is right for the relationship; you may only be seeking that which makes you feel good or happy. However, communicating emotions and desires are still important because they give us understanding into the values that we hold most deeply.

Truly knowing your values comes from comparing them to sacrificial love so you can determine if they are right or wrong. In non-moral areas of life, knowing your values according to the three areas of desire will help you communicate the deeper issues of your heart. Discussion using the framework of sacrificial love and the three areas of desire will also make it easier for you to communicate in words that another person can easily understand.

Especially in times of conflict, seek to list and communicate the values that are driving your desires and choices. You still may not agree with each other because each one of you will place greater preference on different values. However, you will understand one another better and you will more clearly communicate with one another.

If you have a child, attempt to understand the values that are behind his desires and actions. Talk to him about the values that he holds, and discuss how they are like or unlike yours. Teaching your child that relationships are based on common value systems will help him understand the nature of his relationship with you, but it will also prepare him for having better relationships throughout life.

Help your child understand the three areas of desire that he will face in life so that he can make choices that will be best for his relationships with others rather than only for himself. Children care deeply about what others think of them, even more than we who are older do. They need to know that it is better to be good than to satisfy bodily appetites, to have people like them, or to be wealthy or powerful.

Sacrificial love can change you, it can change your child, and it can change the world. As you and your child talk about values and how to sacrificially love those in your family, your family relationships will grow strong. Your family will share an identity of love that will be attractive to all those who live in conflict and heartbreak.

If you do not raise your child to share a common value system with you, he will likely choose one different than yours. That may lead to relational conflict—because all conflict in relationship is conflict over value system. Remember, you do not have to agree on everything. Rather, it is the foundation of sacrificial love that is most important. If you seek to live sacrificially for one another, the other areas of interests that differ will not disturb the peace you share on the deepest level.

7 Becoming a sacrificial lover

The concepts in this book are not difficult to understand, but changing your value system can be very difficult. We like our desires and values, even though we do not always like the results of them. We also prefer that other people change their values to match ours rather than change ourselves.

It can be extremely difficult to practice sacrificial love. You must understand that you cannot merely stop doing selfish things without replacing them with sacrificial actions. The only way to permanently break bad habits is to replace them with good ones. Even though we might be convinced that sacrificial love will transform our relationships, we still struggle with selfishness and fear.

You were created to live in great relationships, yet relational pain is the worst kind of pain in life. Only by living sacrificial love can we undo the damage that we have caused in our relationships. Being successful in loving others sacrificially requires a commitment beyond the current relationship. Since sacrificial love for the benefit of others is God's value system, living it requires his help.

Since all relationship is based on common value systems, deliberately choosing a value system that is different from God's is a choice to limit relationship with him. To reject God's value system is to reject him. The essence of sin is choosing a value system other than God's. It began with mankind's choice to decide for ourselves what is right and wrong. The result of that choice was a breaking of relationship with God.

Not only did we lose our relationship with God, we also damaged our relationships with one another. From the moment we chose our own value systems, we began having conflict with each other, we began blaming each other for our problems, and we began hiding our true values from each other.

The consequence of not sharing a common value system with God is death: separation and broken relationship. Yet God put his own value system into practice by having his own Son experience death for us. God's value system is sacrificial love for the benefit of others, and it was exemplified when Jesus Christ died on the cross. God put the relational consequences of our rebellion (in choosing our own value systems) on Christ. Jesus' relationship with God was broken so that we could experience life and restored relationship with God.

However, Jesus could not remain dead and out of relationship with his Father because they perfectly share the same value system. Jesus rose from the dead and promises eternal salvation to all those who trust that their relationship with God can be restored through his death and resurrection.

God did his value system toward us by having his Son die as a sacrifice of love given to help us. Jesus' death allows us to enter into relationship with God even though we had previously chosen value systems different from his. Through a restored relationship with God based on his treatment of us in sacrificial love, we gain the motivation and power to live his value system.

God did his value system for us at the cross and he asks us to live that same value system for one another. We are to love others by considering their needs before our own and by forgiving them when they hurt us. When Jesus died on the cross he gave up his bodily appetites, having people like him, and all power, wealth, and control. If we want to have our relationships improve, we need to be willing to sacrifice as well.

As in human relationships, resolving your relationship issues with God involves the four steps to an agreement on values. First, you must confess that your value system is not like his. Second, you must repent of choosing selfish values and then adopt God's value system of sacrificial love. Third, you need to ask God to forgive you—something he will gladly do. And fourth, you need to be reconciled to God. That means you need to continue to seek relationship with him based on his value system and enter into the community of all those who share his value system.

Christ's death on the cross allows for a change in our relationship with God, but it also reveals the value system that can fix all of mankind's relational problems. If all human relationships and interactions were based on sacrificial love for others there would be no more war or exploitation. People would care for the environment and seek to help raise those in need out of their poverty.

Sacrificial love takes commitment and faith. It is the value system that can make the world a better place, beginning with you, your family, and your friends. You do not need to believe in Christ to benefit from practicing his value system. However, being involved in a community of people who share this common value system will enable you to understand and live it as God intended.

When people come to Jesus, they either come seeking something *from* him or seek to become *like* him. Discipleship is an issue of becoming like the one you follow—the Master. Jesus taught that he wanted people to become like him and adopt his value system of sacrificial love. Faith in Christ is believing that he loves you and that you demonstrate your love for him in how you love others.

Jesus invited people to enter the spiritual Kingdom of God. If you are not part of the Kingdom of God, then you have not taken the step of committing yourself to follow God's value system of sacrificial love. Desiring to have God's value system as your own is a requirement for entering the Kingdom. Commitment to following God's value system is important for change, because change is fundamental to improving your relationships.

In God's Kingdom there is only one rule: to love one another sacrificially. The consequence of breaking that rule is forgiveness. This is how God treats all those in his Kingdom, and it is how all those in the Kingdom are to treat one another. Only in God's Kingdom will you obtain strength from God to move from a selfish value system to one of sacrificial love.

Living sacrificially all the time is very difficult. We have habits and desires that can only change as we continuously practice God's value system. You need to be part of a community of people who are also committed to living a life of sacrificial love. They will encourage you and help you understand how to love as God does.

In order to improve your relationships, you will need teaching and encouragement to become a sacrificial lover. Your knowledge of God's value system will grow as you read the New Testament and learn what sacrificial love is like when lived out in relationships. However, God does not expect us to live by a list of rules and laws. If we understand sacrificial love properly, and desire to live it, we will begin to do good things for others and avoid doing them harm. That is why anyone who is truly teaching about God's value system will not exploit you.

People have many different ideas of what it means to grow closer to God, but when these ideas are wrong or incomplete it leads to conflict. The only measure of relationship is how much two people agree on value system. This is no different in your relationship with God. Knowing God is an issue of how much you share his value system of sacrificial love. Many people think that God has a long list of rules for them to follow, but actually he only seeks to have one main value take root in our hearts. If our deepest held value is sacrificial love for the benefit of others, all of how we treat others will be positively affected, and we will experience the kinds of relationships that God intends us to have.

Jesus died on the cross to forgive our sins, and faith alone brings salvation; however, seeking forgiveness of sin is always about the desire to restore relationship with the one you have offended and never merely about avoiding punishment. To want the benefits of relationship with God requires a commitment to relationship that exists on truth: a relationship based on God's value system of sacrificial love for the benefit of others.

Additional information and resources on this topic can be found on the internet at http://godsvaluesystem.com, including information on the books *God's Value System* and *Emotions: Revealing Our Value Systems*.

Darren Twa writes and speaks on how to improve relationships using God's value system.

Breinigsville, PA USA
23 October 2009
226334BV00001B/2/P